POWER BI
DEMYSTIFIED

step by step guide on how to create interactive dashboard and report using power bi

Elijah Falode

Contents

INTRODUCTION

Whether you are a business owner, data analyst, or financial analyst, you would like to collate data easily, analyze it, and share same with your colleague in real-time. You would want to do this with software that is easy to operate and publish data with good visuals in a way that you can understand. Microsoft Power BI allows you to get data from different sources, analyze it, and gives you insights on your business and operational performance. You can share workspaces with your colleagues, and they can easily access the business reports you have prepared. It makes collaboration easy. In this book, you will find out what Power BI is, the features, the benefits, and the functions.

This book also discusses the different versions of Microsoft Power BI – Power BI Server, Desktop, Pro, Premium, and Report Server. You will get to understand the diversity between these versions, their features, benefits, and how to set them up. You can operate these Power BI versions both on cloud and on-premise, depending on the features of the versions. You can also share your workspace with as many people as you want. You will get to understand the Power BI versions, and which one best suits your company's needs.

Power BI also allows you to inquire about your data and gives you answers to your question. This is due to the artificial intelligence feature. It also provides you the insight you need to make informed decisions that impact your company's bottom line in a positive way. Microsoft Power BI can also integrate with other on-premise apps on your device so as to enable you to collate data easily. It operates with natural language so that you won't need the help of an expert to operate it.

If you are looking for an advanced software that is better than your Excel, Power BI is the upgrade you need. This book will guide you on everything you need to know about Power BI, and it gives an easy step-by-step guide on how to install, setup, and use it.

Read on to know more!

CHAPTER 1

UNDERSTANDING POWER BI

As a business analyst, data analyst, or business owner, you know the importance of compiling data and tracking them for the growth of your organization. Are you looking for an advanced way of analyzing your business data, and you need more friendly software that you can easily understand? Perhaps, you need an easier means of collecting data from many sources, and analyzing it. Your requirement demands software that will interpret and analyze your data with attractive visuals that you can easily understand and share with your team and stakeholders. Power BI is the software you need. It is able to get information from multiple sources, filter out the ones you don't need, analyze and present them with attractive visuals, and gives you insights that help you predict the future and make informed decisions for your business. The major function of Power BI is to bring your data to life.

What is Power BI?

Power Bi is an artificial intelligence software which performs intelligence services for businesses. It is a collection of business intelligence tools used by non-technical business users for data visualization, analysis, and evaluation. It pulls data from different sources, interprets, and converts them to understandable

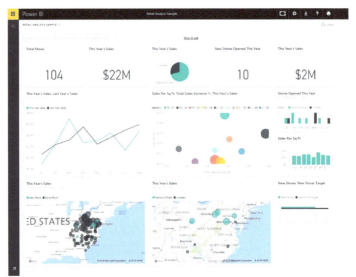

information or insights such as compelling visuals, e.g., graphs and charts. The data it gathers helps users to stay up-to-date with what is going on in their business. Power BI is a Microsoft software. It connects to a range of software like Excel spreadsheet, cloud-based, and on-premise based applications, pulls data from these sources, and creates metrics on your dashboard.

The interface is just like Microsoft Excel; therefore, if you are familiar with Excel, you won't have a hard time operating and understanding how Microsoft Power BI works.

Versions of Power BI

Power BI can work on desktop, Android, and iOS. You can choose from various versions depending on your budget, need, and deployment procedures. You can select either free versions or paid versions based on what suits your needs.

The Power BI Desktop: This version is intended for small to medium-sized businesses, and it is free as well.

Power BI Service: This is in two forms- Power BI Pro and Power BI premium, and both are not free for use. Power BI Pro offers a pay-per-use license service that enables you to gain access to advanced features and the ability to share data. At the same time, Power BI premium offers licenses for scale service and is intended for large-scale businesses and enterprises.

Power BI Mobile: This works on mobile phones and tablets.

Power BI Embedded: This is an embedded version of Power BI, and can be used by independent software developers can put in their app.

Power BI Report Server: It is an on-premise app for businesses who want to keep their reports and data on their server.

Benefits of Power BI

- Power BI works well with known business management tools like Mailchimp, Office 365, Google Analytics, Salesforce, SharePoint, etc., making data collection easy.
- The built-in features help you to track valuable trends that can help you to make educated predictions.
- Power BI can process extensive data that other platforms may find difficult to do efficiently.
- Power BI offers different templates that are used to visualize information efficiently and help you understand your data better.

- Power BI provides strong data security, ensures that your data are safe using granular controls on internal and external accessibility.
- Since the software is cloud-based and operates with artificial intelligence, users get a robust algorithm and intelligent, cutting-edge information.
- The interface enables you to access the information you require quickly without wasting time, making it less complicated than spreadsheets.
- Power BI enables you to connect your data easily.
- You can inquire about your data and get response to your inquiries.

Functions of Power BI

Power BI serves different functions that are beneficial to the growth of your company. These functions are:

Extract and visualize data

Power BI can be used to extract data from different sources, analyze them, and present them in understandable visual forms like pie charts, maps, or bar charts.

Synchronize data

Power BI enables you to get your data from different sources, both on the cloud and on your device and connect them together. You can then convert them to reports that give you insights relating to your business performance. It supports more than 70 connections, gets your data in one place, and allows you easy access to those data.

More advanced analytics

The Power BI possesses features that enable you to perform advanced data analytics functions than other software like Excel.

Collaboration

Power BI functions as a collaboration tool in a way that it makes sharing of data among users easy and enables them to easily access these data. It also offers high security and protective measure at the same time. Users can work together, access the same data at the same time, without bothering about losing vital information to third parties. Different departments can use this to share important information in an organization.

Who needs Power BI?

Due to its function as a business intelligence software, you may quickly assume that data scientists, business analysts, and those in financial need the software more. However, due to its friendly user interface(UI) and convenience, the tool can be used by a range of people in different sectors of business.

Power BI can be used to share data and information in your organization. Anyone can use it depending on their role in your organization or on the workspace, and the data they want to access. It is primarily used by business intelligence professionals to source data, interpret it, and then share it throughout the organization they work for. It is most popular in research, finance, human resources, development, sales, research, and development, as well as marketing departments. Every organization also needs Power BI because it will help them to track growth and efficiency in their organization.

Department reps and managers need Microsoft Power BI to create reports and forecasts that will aid sales and marketing in an organization. They also need it to provide data on how employees and the department are progressing towards achieving the organization's goals. Power BI administrators also need the tool to configure its implementation, as well as monitor its usage and licenses.

Power BI aids easier collation of data from different sources, more advanced analytic functions, and better visual representation of your insights. It has many benefits over other data collection software and gives you insights on trends and algorithm, which helps you make informed decisions for your company. It is a better upgrade for you if you are a finance professional, data analyst, or business analyst.

Now, let's look at the components of Power BI in the next chapter.

CHAPTER 2

THE COMPONENTS OF POWER BI

The pace at which technology is advancing in this dispensation has made the operation of visualization, analysis, sharing, transformation, and modeling of data less difficult and easily accessible. Among which is the launching of Power BI, which is a self-service business analytical tool.

Business Intelligence users and other organizations find the tool useful because of the following features:

Reports: The data collected in a visual manner consisting of various pages are referred to as reports.

Visualization: In Power BI, data represented in a pictorial manner is termed visualizations.

Tiles: These are single pictures on the dashboard.

Datasets: This consists of the visual-like data represented in Power BI.

Dashboard: The number of graphic images in Power BI is contained here.

Components of Power Bi

The components of Power BI include;

- Power Pivot
- Power Map
- Power Query
- Power BI Questions and Answers
- Data Catalog
- Power View
- Data Management Gateway
- Power Bi Mobile App
- Power BI Website

Power Pivot

This is an add-in utilized for calculating and modeling easy and compound data. It makes handling large sizes of data sets easier for customizing and making flexible into Excel package. With the aid of Power Pivot, by just dragging and dropping method, software packages such as hierarchies, custom measures, KPIs, and relationships can be created.

Furthermore, Power Pivot is used majorly for calculations, and the language used is *Data Analysis Expression (DAX)*.

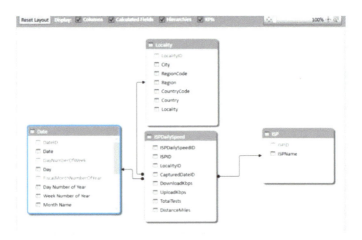

Power Map

The map is used for visualizing data by representing it on a geographic map. The data is pictured in a 3D model, and once this is done, it showcases it in another dimension quite different from the former, which implies that there'll be a need to convert from pictorial to a geographical map view.

One of the features of Power Map is that the length of a column can be figured out in a way different from the original. You can arrive at the best of Power Map when you connect it to the Bing Maps, depending on the data gathered from the state, address, country, or city.

Power Query

This appears to be one of the essential constituents of Power BI. It can be used as a part of Power BI Desktop and can also be included in Excel. Its major elements are accessing, searching, and transformation of data from public sources.

With the aid of Power Query, you can generate data from several sources of data and as well garner data from a huge range of databases such as MySQL, Oracle, SQL, and a host of many others.

Data can as well be retrieved from records such as Excel files, CSV files, and text files. It also helps to find data from social media sites, including open data and big data, making the data readable and for it to also perform other functions like merging in Excel.

The language used by Power Pivot is Power Query M Formula Language. This package consists of diverse components that are not easily accessible by a GUI.

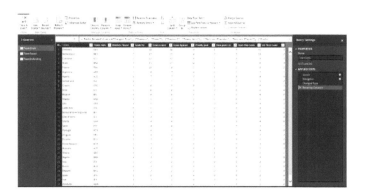

Power View

This is the main data capturing feature of Power BI. It helps to develop and buttresses more points on animation, charts, diagrams, graphs, and many more instead of unnecessarily adding up to the rows and columns of the data.

It is an interactive part of Power BI that gains direct access to data sources and recovers data for the purpose of analysis.

You can use Slicers to dissect data in Power BI.

Data Management Gateway

This helps to join data to the cloud found on the premises. Immediately the data gains access into the cloud; it quickly reacts to the datasets and reveals the graphic images as fast as possible.

DMG is an easy way to periodically refresh data, and the data fields are easily reflected, tables are also exposed.

Power BI Questions and Answers

Power BI Q&A is a simple language format used for asking data model questions and getting answers to the questions. In order to arrive at this, you are expected to create a pictorial space in your data and tag it Questions and Answer.

After you must have gathered your data model and updated it on the Power BI site, then you are expected to ask questions if you've got any, and solutions will be proferred almost immediately. These questions could be represented on a map for prompt accessibility.

Data Catalog

They can be used to carry out the search function on the Power BI, figure out queries and find prompt solutions to them.

Power BI Mobile App

This consists of three mobile operating system providers- iOS, Windows, and Android. On the Power BI website, these applications give room for a responsive view of reports and dashboards. The mobile app is sharable, so also is the report.

Game Results.pbix

Updated just now

Goals scored

by Team

Completed Clearances, Saves

by Team

21

Power BI Website

Reports which can be shared with other users can be created on the Power BI websites. With the use of a web browser, one can carry out slice and dice operations online. This does not require the need to use any tool whatsoever.

CHAPTER THREE

FEATURES OF POWER BI

Data happens to be the heart of every business. In the meantime, falsification of facts happens to be one of the challenges faced by various organizations in recent times. When you talk about Power BI, it automatically implies the tool that makes room for easy analysis of data. This makes Power BI, which is an exceptional and vigorous intelligence tool to become the best tool suitable for data modeling and representation, which has come to stay in the world of data sources. It is helpful such that it provides multiple sources of data to get connected as fast as possible and also helps to permeate life into the data via wide-ranging reports.

Features of Power BI

Multiple Data Sources

This suite makes it easy for Power BI users to select from a series of other data sources. The data ranges from structured to unstructured, on-premise to cloud-based. Among the latest available data sources are PDF, Azure, SQL Server, Excel, MySQL database, Power BI dataflows, CSV, Oracle, Power BI dataflows, etc.

Datasets Filtration

This is a single dataset arrived at after gathering data from different sources. The datasets can be used to manufacture various sets of visualizations. What Power BI does in this instance is that it makes the provision of a huge range of data connectors such as SQL database, Facebook, MailChimp, Excel, Salesforce, and several others for its users. This makes it easy for the users to connect to several data sources in order to create datasets by way of importing data from one or several other sources.

Data Analysis Expression (DAX) function

The DAX functions are predefined codes that perform analytics specific functions on data. There are about two hundred Data Analysis Expression functions in the Power BI system.

Customized Dashboards

Dashboards are a range of diverse visualizations that provide meaningful intuitions into data. A distinctive Power Bi dashboard is a composition of diverse pictorials such as tiles. The dashboard can be shared between two or more sources.

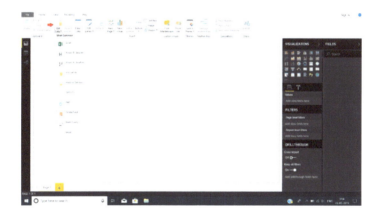

Flexible Tiles

This is a solitary block that comprises visualization in a Power BI dashboard. In order to get a clearer view of the pictures, titles help to separate the various set of information. It is important to note, however, that the tiles can be changed, and the size can also be accustomed. Depending on the choice of the users, tiles can be positioned and relocated anywhere on the dashboard.

Navigation Pane

This constitutes such options as dashboards, reports, and datasets. It makes it easy for users to be able to navigate between the dashboards they are working on, the reports they are creating, and the datasets also.

Attractive Visualisations

This refers to the pictorial representation of data in Power BI. It can be used to create dashboards and reports either as compound or easy visualization, just the way you want it appeared on your dashboard. There are series of customized graphic images that can be created on Power BI; a few among them are Ribbon chart, Area chart, Stacked bar chart, Line chart, Clustered column chart, 100% stacked column chart, Map, Funnel chart, Pie chart, Waterfall

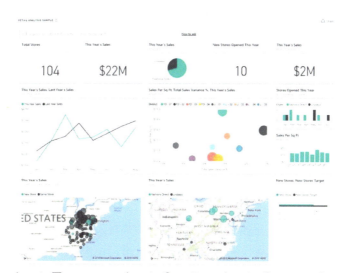

chart, Treemap chart, Scatter chart, Guage chart and a host of many others.

Informative Reports

This depicts a detailed representation of both structured and complete data representations displayed on the dashboard showing important information from the data. Reports can be shared conveniently from one user to the other.

Feedback/Help Buttons

Once these buttons are clicked on, they automatically direct users to different option settings such as giving reports to the Power BI team, requesting funding and succor, downloading, etc.

Office 365 Application Launcher

This suite enables users to launch Microsoft Office 365 apps conveniently.

The Natural Language Question and Answer Box

This is one of the important features of Power BI. It helps the customer to express themselves by making as much enquiries about information that they would like to know. These questions are, however, asked in natural language because it easily helps them to identify the unique insight contained in the Power BI structure. The cognitive engine makes use of suggestions, rephrasing autofill, and other techniques to provide answers to the questions asked by the users.

Importance of Power BI

Power BI is of utmost importance in business settings as it helps to create information, execute plans, read data on a wide range of business priorities.

- It helps to share data faster and conveniently within a short space of time among users in the organization.
- It helps you to control and display the data in use.
- Business analysts make use of Power BI to model and customize data without stress.
- Power BI can be used to gain access to real-time analytics in order for you to get connected to the flow of data in your organization and to as well partake in another decision making.
- It aids in the optimization of machine learning replicas.
- With the aid of Power BI, you will enjoy a free flow of collaboration in your organizational setup.

Power BI is a software that comprises multiple collections of Business Intelligence tools, including data connectors, applications, and software services. It is a cloud-based network used to garner data from numerous sources.

So how do you begin with the Power BI Services? Read on!

CHAPTER 4

GETTING STARTED WITH POWER BI SERVICE

The Power BI service is sometimes referred to as Power BI online because it is a platform built upon the Azure Cloud platform and adheres to HTML5 standards. It is a Software as a service (SaaS) version of Microsoft Power BI. This software gives you insight leveraging on the data it sources, and provides information that serves your business effectively.

Datasets for Power BI service

Power BI service datasets are a set of data you can connect to or import. Power BI allows you to have your data together in one place so that you can easily access it. You can group your datasets into different workspaces depending on the purpose of each workspace. You can also have a dataset in different workspaces. Workspaces are holders for reports, workbooks, dashboards, dataflows, datasets, and reports in Power BI, and they are in two forms; My workspace and workspaces. Only you have access to My workspace, while you can share workspaces with your colleagues. You can keep datasets in any of these workspaces or both.

There are many datasets that are supported by Microsoft Power BI like Excel workbook, SSAS tabular dataset, Salesforce dataset, etc. Datasets can be renamed, refreshed, or removed by anyone who has access to the workspace, be it admin, contributor, or member. If you want to connect to a dataset, click on "Get Data" at the bottom of the navigation panel, then you can get the data you want from its source.

You can also access your dataset from My workspace or any of the workspaces you have used them. Also, visualization of one dataset can display on different desktop as long as it is being used.

Features of Power BI service

The features of the Power BI service are the elements you will see when you open your Power BI service app. The features include:

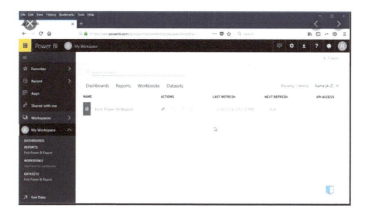

- Navigation pane
- Power BI home button
- Icon buttons, plus settings, help, and feedback
- Microsoft 365 app launcher
- Recent dashboards, reports, and workspaces
- Search box
- Your workspaces: My workspace and workspaces
- Favorite and frequent dashboards, reports, and workspaces

Benefits of Power BI service

Integrates existing app easily: It integrates well with your existing business analytics apps to get data.

Detailed and personalized dashboard: The dashboard is designed in a user-friendly way that can be personalized to do your work and that of your team easier on the app. You can customize the dashboard in a way that best suits your need.

Publish reports securely: It publishes the reports of your data securely in a manner that you and other users can view them on different dashboards. Power BI service allows you to also refresh data reports.

No speed and memory constraint: Power BI service is fast and publishes reports with speed. It is also a cloud-based software, so data can be easily retrieved or analyzed without fear of you losing your data.

No specialized technical supports required: It backs a strong natural language interface. Therefore, it can be operated easily without the help of technical supports. It also uses intuitive graphical designer tools, which makes data analysis easy to understand by users.

The balance between simplicity and performance: It is an effective way of collecting data from multiple sources and analyzing data with an utmost degree of simplicity. The reports are usually not complicated to understand, and at the same time, it doesn't publish mediocre reports. Power BI service's simplicity and performance are efficient, and they are both balanced.

Supports advanced data services: Microsoft Power BI service tools can work together with other advanced cloud services like Cortana or Bot and produce results in natural language that will be easily understood by users.

How to get started with Power BI service

Before you get started on the Power BI service, you need to have signed up on Microsoft Power BI. If you don't have an account, sign up for a Power BI pro free trial or a paid one if you can afford it. After you have signed up for the Pro trial, you can get started.

Step 1: Get Data

- First, sign in to your Power BI profile, and

- Click "my workspace" visible on the navigation pane.

- Select new, then upload a new file. This opens the "Get data" page.

- Select the file under the "create a new content section."

- Browse through the files on your computer to select the exact one you need and open, import, or upload it on your Power BI workspace.

- Once your dataset is ready, click on the "More options (…)" next to "Financial Sample dataset" and select "Create a report."

- Then, open the report editor

- This means that you are in the editing view. You can also switch to reading view at the top bar after you're done editing. Because you are the owner of the workspace, you view it in editing mode, and when you share it with your colleagues, they can only view it in the reading mode because you're the creator and owner of the report.

Step 2: Create Chart Report

You are now connected to data, so you can start exploring the Power BI service. These are the steps on how to create a chart report:

- Since you are in the editor's view, commence in the "Fields" pane located on the right part of the page to create a visualization. Choose the "Gross Sales" field, then click on the "Date" field. Some fields under the "Fields" section have Sigma symbols beside them because Power BI sensed that they contain numbers.

- Select the visualization of your data, how you want it to be displayed.

- You can pin any of the data visualizations to any of the dashboard you like.

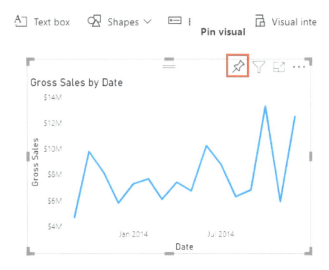

- Because it's a new report, you have to save the visualization before you can save it on a dashboard. Therefore, give your report a name and save it. This means that you are now viewing it in reading view.
- Select the "pin" icon, and select "new dashboard," and give it any name you like.

You can change the visualization anytime you want, but the one you pinned on a different dashboard doesn't change. If you keep updating your data on your dashboard, it changes the report in the visualization you saved.

- If you want to change back the view to editing view, click on "More options (…)" at the top bar of your dashboard and choose "edit".

Step 3: Explore with Q & A

Now that you're done exploring the chart reports explore the Q & A as well. The Q & A section enables you to ask questions regarding your data using natural language and get a response to your questions. The Q & A section is above your dashboard "Ask a question about your data," below the menu bar.

- First, you go back to your dashboard by clicking on "my workspace" on the Power BI header bar.

- On "my workspace," click on "dashboard."

- Click on the Q & A box that contains "ask a question about your data." It automatically brings suggestions about questions you can ask. If it doesn't suggest questions, switch on "New Q & A Experience."

- Q & A presents your answer in card visualization, which you can pin to a dashboard—select pin visual.

You should explore other things on your Power BI service account, like repositioning tiles. Exit the Q & A and return to your dashboard.

Step 4: Reposition tiles

One interesting thing you can do on the Power BI service is repositioning your tiles in a way that suits you or permits easy navigation.

- You can drag your visuals and arrange them so that they fit together.

- Choose the tile you want to move, pull it till you it gets to your desired spot, and release it.

- If you've arranged visualizations together, you can rename them so that you won't confuse them or mix them up.

- This brings out the details of the tiles, then you can edit the title of the tile.

- Select "more options (…)" and click edit details.

Step 5: Clean up Resources

Now that you are done exploring the features and parts of your Power BI service dashboard, you have to clear the dataset, reports, and dashboard to start properly.

- Select "my workspace" on the Power BI header.
- Select the "more option (…)" and click on "delete."

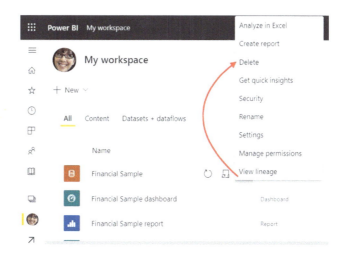

Now that you understand how to use the Microsoft Power BI service, you can get started on your projects and start tracking and analyzing data that will help your business to function more efficiently.

CHAPTER 5

Power BI Desktop

Power BI Desktop which is also referred to as Power BI Free is a free desktop app that can be installed on a local computer. One of its features is that it enables you to transform, connect, and have your data in pictorial form. It works hand in hand with the Power BI service to make shaping, creation of reports, and exploration of advanced data available for users' sake.

Power BI Desktop makes it easier for you to save your report in a file and have both your data and report published on your Power BI website for easy accessibility and uncomplicated "shareability." You can find Power BI Free on all Office 365 Plans, and you can as well sign up to the site at any given time.

Business analysts make use of Power BI Desktop to create several kinds of reports and then go ahead to share these reports with the use of Power BI service.

However, you can make use of Power BI Desktop to connect to diverse sources of data, modeling them into a data prototype.

Why Power BI Desktop?

- The desktop will be able to display as many graphic images as you desire and it also organizes and serves as a cleanser for data.
- With the aid of Power BI, you or your company will be able to refresh your work a maximum of eight times on a daily basis, either hourly or in between working hours.
- People who use desktop have access to a total of 10GB storage in the Power BI cloud, and they are at freedom to upload up to 1GB at once.
- Desktop permits you to get your Power BI connected to multiple sources of data without any form of restrictions except for the quantity of data you can feed in and the amount you can upload at a particular period in time.
- With the use of desktop, users are liable to gain entire access to the visualization templates of Power BI.

- Also, you will be granted access to move your reports and data to Excel.

Note

One important thing needed to note about Power BI Desktop is the fact that it doesn't allow you to share data with your other users. The only thing you will be able to do on it is to have the reports published on the internet, which will be made public for other users to access after some time. This is, however, not ideal when one is dealing with registered business data.

Features of Power BI Desktop

- **It is easier and faster**: Immediately you sign up on the Power BI Desktop, you'll automatically be in charge of your data without the need for any formal training, credit card, setup, or any other thing you may want to think of. Out-of-the-box-dashboards such as Google Analytics, Salesforce, and Dynamics provide you more information from your data within the twinkle of an eye.
- **Provides prompt response to your doubt**: With Power BI Desktop, you can ask questions in natural language and get

the appropriate visualizations in the mode of graphs and charts for your answer.

- **It helps you to make absolute data decisions:** No matter where you find yourself, you will have access to all your data on Android, iOS, and Windows.
- **It ensures accuracy:** No matter where you are and the amount of data you've got to analyze, with the use of on-premises databases, streaming data, cloud services, and Excel spreadsheets, you end up getting accurate results for your enterprise.
- **Allows you to air your idea on your site:** With Power BI Desktop, you gain the chance to reach out to millions of people who make use of any device in any part of the world.

Benefits of Power BI Desktop

As your business expands, you'll find difficulty managing the organization's data. This will go a long way, restraining the business from growing as expected, hence, causing fallbacks for its future dealings. In a way to avert such, smarter business intelligence should be incorporated for effective data analysis; hence, the need for Power BI Desktop.

Power BI Desktop is a cloud-based tool that does not require any funding or infrastructural backing, not minding the bigness or smallness of the business. The users of this tool do not necessarily have to go undergo any formal training, and the current recapitulation of the tool does not necessitate legacy software package limitations.

Its benefits include;

- Power BI Desktop helps you to publish your reports steadily. This allows all the users to gain access to up-to-date information.
- There is no limit to the speed and amount of data it can contain
- It goes hand in hand with other apps that have been in existence in your business without stress.
- It features a detailed personalized dashboard that can be restructured to meet the expectations of any organization.
- It doesn't require any external technical know-how because it makes use of graphical designer tools, and the only language it understands is natural language.
- It helps your enterprise to make timely data decisions. This is achieved via the transformation of your organization's data

into rich visualization, hence, mining business intelligence.

- With the use of natural language, it provides strong backing for data services through advanced cloud services such as Bot Framework, Cortana, or Cognitive services.

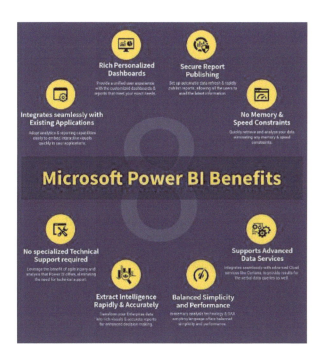

How to Get Started with Power BI Desktop

Power BI Desktop helps to integrate visual techs, data modeling, and a proven Microsoft query engine. It brings together and does easy works that have been considered unorganized and disconnected. Also, processes design and creates smart business intelligence reports.

It is, however, important to note that there is a special version of POWER BI referred to as Power BI Report Server with the main aim of reporting and data analysis. Follow the steps below to start making use of your Power BI Desktop.

Install and launch Power BI Desktop

You can access this from the Power BI Desktop download page. Once you click on the page and it pops up, the next thing you should do is to click on "Download free." Also, you can install Power BI Desktop via Power BI Service. All you'll have to do is, click on the Download icon in the topmost menu bar and select Power BI Desktop. On the MS Word page, click "Get" and then install Power BI Desktop on your CPU.

Connect to data

Once you have the Power BI Desktop installed on your laptop, you automatically have access to connecting to sources of data around the world. In order to view different types of data, click on

Get data > More in the Home tab and then move through all lists of the entire data sources. In the process, you'll discover that you have gotten connected to various sources of Web data.

Adjust your data

Now that you have been connected to a variety of data sources, you can now shape the data to your utmost desire.

You can do this by making provision for Power Query Editor with step by step guidelines on how to adjust the data while you load and present it.

Build Your Reports

It is now time for you to build your report. It is important, however, to note that in Power BI Desktop Review, one can build visuals and reports at the same time.

Components of the Report

The report has six major parts, which include:

- The ribbon is found at the topmost, and it indicates common tasks in view with visualizations and reports.
- The canvas located in the middle, where pictorials are designed and put in order

- The pages tab at the bottom which is for the purpose of adding report pages
- The filters pane which is used to filter data visualizations
- The field pane shows the total fields available in your queries.

Distribute your report

Now that your Power BI Desktop is ready, you can now share it with other users. This can be done in many ways. It can be uploaded, distributed, or directly published via Power BI Desktop to Power BI service.

In sum, Power BI Desktop can be connected to a diagnostic port. This port gives room for other tools to get connected and carry out traces for diagnostic sake.

It is important to bear in mind that when you're making use of the diagnostics port, you may not be able to make further changes to the model, this is because making changes on the port may eventually lead to loss of data and corruption of files.

CHAPTER 6

WHAT IS POWER BI PRO?

Power BI Pro is a user license that allows you, as a user to read and relate with other users' works and information that have been in the Power BI service printed work. As a Power BI Pro user, you are authorized to share and participate with other users on the Power BI Pro service. The right to publish, share and collaborate with other users is exclusive to Power BI Pro users; the exception to this rule only occurs if it is Power BI Premium that is in charge of the content. Power BI Pro has dual functionality, which lets you make use of it individually or as a group. This means you can use Power BI Pro as your individual data analysis of visualization tool, or you can use it to carry out group activities.

With Power Bi Pro, you can share reports within Microsoft tools such as SharePoint, PowerPoint, or other productivity tools. It offers two

51

submissions as an operational SaaS; the tools are Power BI Desktop (for generating information) and Native mobile BI apps (for intermingling with information on Android devices and iOS. Power BI Pro is a great tool for businesses and organizations that make use of Power BI heavily for data creation and wish to do more by sharing and consuming data, reports, and dashboards with other users. Workers across different units can collaborate with other workers through Power BI Pro to report, share and make use of data among themselves.

Functions of Power BI Pro

Below are the many possibilities you can achieve with Power BI Pro.

It helps you collaborate with other users.

Power BI Pro lets you share, distribute data, dashboards, and reports among other users in the Power BI Pro circle. By sharing and interacting with resources among users, Power BI Pro gives every user to learn, collaborate and make informed decisions.

It gives you access to knowledge at your fingertips.

Power BI Pro lets you ask questions from like-minds and get answers quickly. With Power BI Pro, you are able to learn new things and more about the things you already know through your liberty to consume other user's content. With Power BI Pro pre-built data visualizations and reports template, you are able to get access to receiving news on things you are most interested in and things that are most relevant to you.

It helps you do more with tools you already know.

With Power BI Pro, you can get more done with tools you are most familiar with. For instance, you can share your reports and data with tools your staff members and co-workers use every day, such as Dynamics 365, Microsoft Power Platforms, and more. You can also do more with sharing and learning with the different types of software you are already comfortable with, such as Azure, Excel, and more through the Power BI Pro.

It helps you protect your data.

Power BI Pro helps you protect your data, so you don't lose them through role-specific data protection and ow-level security.

How to get started with Power BI Pro

Once you've signed up with Power BI service through the steps mentioned in chapter 4, getting started with Power BI Pro would be very easy because as you explore the Power BI service, you would begin to receive pop-up messages requesting if you would like to upgrade to power BI Pro 60 days individual free trial. If you would like to upgrade, select **"start trial"** as seen in the image below.

Free Trial Expiration

After 60 days, your free individual access to Power BI Pro expires, and your license changes back to the Power BI free license you were using before you upgraded, after which you would no longer have access to use Power BI Pro license anymore. If you wish to continue with Power BI, select **buy now** as in the image below.

CHAPTER 7

POWER BI PREMIUM

Power BI Premium is the most expensive version of Microsoft Power BI. It allows you to license per capacity of your Power BI contents; dashboards, datasets, and reports. That is, rather than pay perusers that have access to the dashboards, datasets, and reports, you pay per the capacity of the contents on your account. By doing this, other users you share your content with can only view the contents and not edit it or create new content. You can share your content with as many users as possible without paying extra cost perusers, but you as the creator need your Power BI Pro license. You can as well make payment for every user, which is a relatively new option. Power BI Premium also allows you to combine with on-premise apps on your device.

Power BI premium is good for you if you:

- Have large sets of contents; datasets, reports, and dashboards. Since you pay per capacity, you enjoy increased storage and performance capabilities.
- Have a large number of users. It will save you the cost of paying perusers, and all your connected users get to have access to contents.
- Use embedding in custom applications.
- Aren't ready to move all your reports to the cloud and would like to combine your Power BI software with on-premise SQL server reporting services.

Benefits of Power Bi Premium

Power BI premium is very flexible and offers a number of advantages, and allows you to share and collaborate with as many users as possible with more capacity to contain your contents.

- It is more cost-effective that as many as 500 users can have access to your content without paying per user.

You can have larger datasets on your Power BI software because you are left with no option than to pay per capacity.

- Greater refresh frequency – you can refresh your data as many times as possible, unlike another version of Power BI, where you have eight days refreshing limit.

- Embedded reports

- On Power BI premium, tools like DAX Studio, SQL Server Management Studio, Power BI Desktop, etc., can connect to your datasets.

- You can connect your Power BI premium to third party applications.

Power BI Premium Capabilities

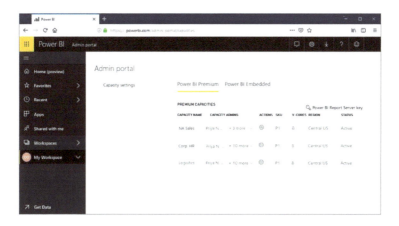

- Larger scale and presentation for your Power BI reports
- Suppleness to license by capacity
- It reports data with amazing data visualization and insights.
- It supports combining self-service and enterprise Power BI with Premium capabilities for heavier workloads.
- It has a built-in license that extends on-premise Power BI and on-premise Power BI Report Server.
- It supports regional location data and customer-managed encoding keys for data.

- It has the ability to share your Power BI content with anyone within or outside your organization without purchasing a peruser license.

Features of Power BI Premium

The features of Power BI Premium based on its benefits and capacity are:

- Six capacity models, each with memories that vary; You can pick the memory size you need to run your Power BI platform.
- Ability to store Power BI assets on-premises through Power BI Report Server
- Up to 100 terabytes of data storage
- 50 gigabyte capacity on dataset size

How to Get Started with Power Bi Premium

Getting started with Power BI Premium involves creating, managing, and monitoring Power Bi Premium capacities. The main thing about Power BI Premium is the capacity because it is the resources that are reserved for you for use on Power BI. Here's how you can get started on Power BI premium:

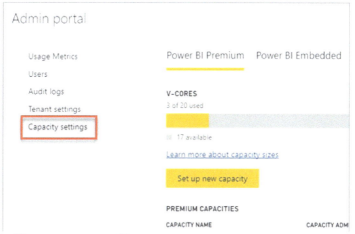

Manage capacity

After you have purchased the capacity you need for your Power BI contents; you manage the capacity in the "Capacity setting" section of the admin portal.

Choose the capacity you intend to manage. After you have selected, it takes you to the management screen. If you are yet to assign a workspace to the capacity, a message will pop up and ask you to assign the capacity to a workspace.

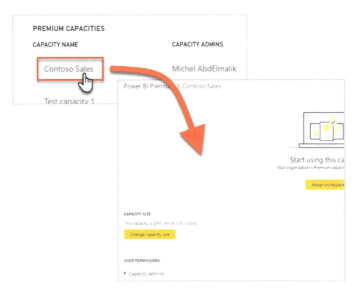

How to Set Up a New Capacity

- First, you need to go to the admin portal. This will show you the quantity of virtual cores (v-cores) in your possession.

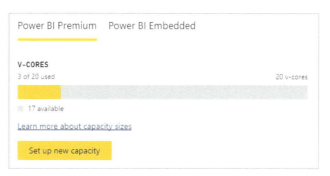

- If there are other v-cores, select "create a new capacity."
- Give a new capacity a name.
- State who the admin of this new capacity is.
- Select the capacity size, depending on the amount you need and the amount you have left.

- Select set up

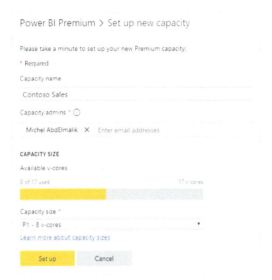

Power BI Premium > Set up new capacity

Please take a minute to set up your new Premium capacity.

* Required

Capacity name

Contoso Sales

Capacity admins * ⓘ

Michel AbdElmalik ✕ Enter email addresses

CAPACITY SIZE

Available v-cores

8 of 17 used   17 v-cores

Capacity size *

P1 - 8 v-cores   ▾

Learn more about capacity sizes

Set up   Cancel

The capacity admins, Power BI admins, and global administrators who have access to your Power BI will be notified, and it will appear in their admin portals.

Capacity setting

- Select actions in the Premium Capacity management screen, and click on the gear icon, or update or change a setting.

ACTIONS	SKU	V-CORES
⚙	P1	8

- There you will see the admins who have access to the capacities, size of the capacity, and the capacity section.

Settings for Contoso Sales

Capacity name

Contoso Sales

SERVICE ADMIN

Colin Murphy	colin@granularcontrols1.onmicros...
Michel AbdElmalık	admin@granularcontrols1.onmicr...
Nancy Leary	nancy@granularcontrols1.onmicr...
Tim Larson	tım@granularcontrols1.onmicroso...

SKU/SIZE

P1

REGION

Central US

- You can delete or rename your capacity.

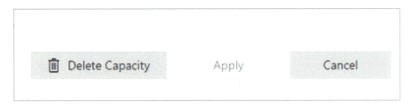

Change capacity size

- Only admins who have access to the capacity can change its size. However, Capacity admins who are not Power BI admins and global administrators cannot change its size.
- Select "Change capacity size."

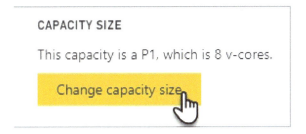

- Increase or reduce the capacity size as you desire.

Manage user permission

As the creator, you can add more capacity admin, user admin and assign them capacity duty authorizations. Users aren't admins but have project approvals can allot a workstation to a capacity if they are admins on the workspace, as well as disperse their individual workplace to the dimensions, but they do not have access to the admin portal.

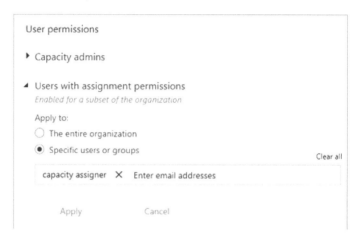

You can manage individual project and allot individuals in the "User permissions" section.

Assigning a workspace to a capacity

- You can do this via the admin board or through a workspace.
- From the admin board, select "assign workspaces."

- Select "apply to." Make your choice and click on "apply."

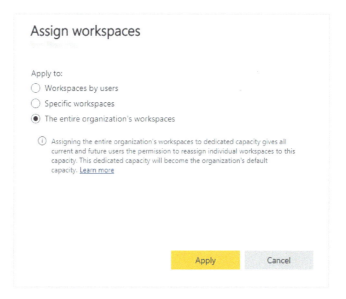

- If you want to allocate from the workplace, select a workplace by selecting the (…) bar by the side, and click on "edit workspace."

- Expand advanced under the "edit workstation," and allocate the workstation to a dimension, and choose "save."

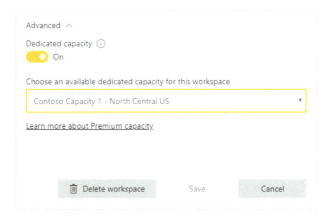

Power BI Report Server product key

Only capacity admins can see this on their Power BI admin board. Only global administrators and users are granted a Power BI service administration role, and users who have purchased a Power BI Premium SKU have access to it.

Select the "Power BI Report Server key" in your admin portal, and a dialog that contains your invention key will be displayed. Copy the product key and use it for the installation.

71

CHAPTER 8

POWER BI REPORT SERVER

Microsoft Power BI Report Server is a presupposed server which helps you to bring about and demonstrate KPIs and reports. It is a server with a web portal which is employed to host Power BI reports. It is also a one-stop service for all your reporting assets in that it allows you to host paginated reports, mobile reports, and KPIs. It is structured like the SQL Server Reporting Services and is used to host Power BI reports on an on-premise server. You can get Power BI Report Server from Power BI Premium or through an active SQL Server Enterprise Software Assurance (SA).

Features of Power Bi Report Server

Can Host Power BI On-premises: It is an on-premise solution used to work in partnership and allocate Power BI reports with other users.

Custom visuals: It can render custom visuals and has up to 100 custom visuals.

Power BI Mobile: It is possible for you to link your Power BI Report Server with your mobile app and view reports on your mobile phone. Power BI mobile app is available on various phone types like android, Ios, Windows phones, etc.

Reports view via the web: you can access data and interact with other users via the web platform. Users can use and apply actions like cross-filtering, explorations of data, tooltips, slicers, etc., on the web.

Export report data to CSV: Users can transfer figures from reports contained on a Report Server to a CSV plan.

Limitations of Power BI Report Server

- Lack of Power BI service features – it only functions as a report server and doesn't have features like dashboards, Q & A, and streaming data.

- No preview features
- Constrained to analysis services
- Users don't get access to dashboards, real-time streaming, and content packs.
- Users don't get access to app offices and ordinary dialectal interrogations.
- Users can't examine data in email subscriptions, Excel, or data signals.
- Power BI Report Server has a sparser update cycle; that is, it is updated every four months rather than a month like the other Power BI versions. New features and fixes are only made every four months.

How to install Power BI Report Server.

You'll be able to install Power BI Report Server in two ways:

- SQL Server Enterprise Software Assurance (SA)

- Power BI Premium

Before you go right ahead to install Power BI Report Server on your computer, these are some of the system requirements that will enable you to download it:

System Requirements

Before you start installing the Report Server, ensure your system is in line with the structure conditions given below:

- You should have any of these platforms – Windows 10/ 8/ 8.1 or Window Server 2012/Window Server 2012R2/ Window Server 2016.

- .NET Framework 4.5.2 or later or a later version

- SQL Server Database Engine 2008 or a later version. It will be beneficial for storage of a report server file.

- A later version or SQL Server Analysis Services 2012 SP1 CU4. This is required for your Live Analysis Services sources of information.

Installing via Power BI Premium

- First, you must have acquired Power BI Premium. In the "Premium setting" section of the Power BI management entry, select the "Power BI Report Server key."
- You can duplicate the key and use it for your fitting.

Installation via SQL Server Enterprise Software Assurance (SA)

- First, copy your key's product from the Volume Licensing Service Centre if you already have a SQL Server Enterprise Software Assurance agreement.
- During installation, it is not necessary that you have SQL Server Database Engine server, but it is necessary for configuring reporting services once installation is done.
- Figure outpower the setting of PowerBIReportServer.exe and unveil the installer. Then, click on "install Power BI Report Server."

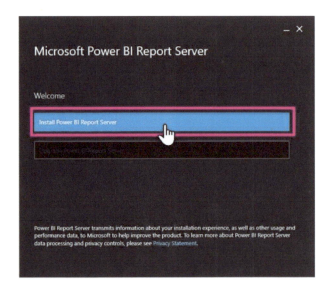

- Choose the edition you intend to install and click on "next."

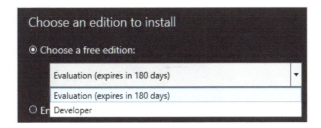

- After selecting the edition, enter the product key that you got from Power BI Premium or the Volume License Centre.
- Read the license terms and conditions and make sure you agree before clicking on "I agree to take the authorization standings," and then select next.

- A Database Engine is necessary to enable you access the database Report Server. Therefore, select an available

Database Engine, then select "Next" to fix the Report Server.

- Select the place you want your Report Server file to be installed in. Click on "install" and continue.

- After setting up, click on "Configure Report Server" to enable you to unveil the Reporting Services Conformation Manager.

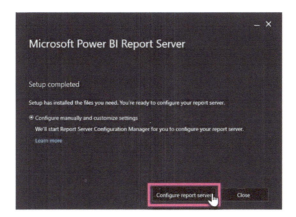

After the configuration of your report server is done, your Microsoft Power BI Report Server is ready for use. This Power BI version has restricted functions mentioned in the limitations section, but it allows you to view your information on-premise.

CONCLUSION

Sourcing data and getting excellent report visualization shouldn't give you a hard time anymore, now that you know more about the Microsoft Power BI. You know what Power BI is, its capabilities, and the benefits your company stand to gain from it. At this juncture, you should know which version of Power Bi suits your company's needs, and you should be getting ready to use it if you haven't started already.

You can try out the trial versions and follow the step-by-step procedures on how you can set up Power BI and operate it. The right business intelligence software you need is Power Bi, and you have a variety of options to pick from.

From all the chapters in this book, you have enough resources that will guide you, help you with your business analysis, and give you insights into all your business efforts. Utilize these resources, and see the difference in your business performance.

ABOUT THE AUTHOR

Elijah Falode is a Top-Rated Content Writer on Upwork and a Professional Content Development Consultant with over ten years of experience in educating people about business and emerging technologies.

In the past five years, he has collaborated and worked with thought leaders and industry experts as a content development consultant.

He has researched, and ghostwritten content on emerging technologies- AI, Voice economy, Big Data, Connected Cloud, RPA, IoT and Cybersecurity, and He is fully aware of their capabilities and risks.

You can follow him on Linkedin @Elijahfalode.

BOOK BY THE AUTHOR

The Future of Intelligent Automation: How AI and RPA can impact your business processes

"Great summary and easy to read book. I recommended it to friends as an intro to the topic of Automation."

MK, United Kingdom

Index

3D model, 18
algorithm, 10, 14
Android, 8, 23, 52, 62
Area chart, 32
artificial intelligence, 5,
  7, 10
Azure Cloud platform,
  36
business analytical
  tool, 15
business analytics
  apps, 39
Business Intelligence,
  15, 34
business intelligence
  tools, 7
business reports, 4
Clustered column
  chart, 32
Cortana, 41, 55
CSV files, 19
dashboard, 1, 8, 16,
  29, 30, 32, 39, 44,
  45, 46, 47, 55
dashboards, 23, 30,
  32, 37, 39, 40, 52,
  62, 66, 67, 84
data, 4, 5, 6, 7, 9, 10,
  11, 12, 13, 14, 15,
  16, 17, 18, 19, 20,
  21, 22, 26, 27, 29,
  32, 34, 36, 37, 39,
  40, 42, 43, 44, 45,

46, 48, 49, 50, 51, 52,
  54, 55, 56, 57, 59,
  60,

61, 62, 63, 64, 68, 69,
  70, 83, 84, 93

Data Analysis
  Expression, 17, 29
data analyst, 4, 6, 14
Data Catalog, i, 16, 23
Data Management
  Gateway, i, 16, 21
data modeling, 26
datasets, 21, 27, 30,
  36, 37, 66, 67, 68
DMG, 21
Excel spreadsheet, 8
Facebook, 27
financial analyst, 4
Funnel chart, 32
Google Analytics, 9,
  52
Guage chart, 32
GUI, 19
iOS, 8, 23, 52, 62
KPIs, 17, 82
Line chart, 32
machine learning, 34
Mailchimp, 9
MailChimp, 27
Map, 18, 32
Microsoft 365, 39

www.ingramcontent.com/pod-product-compliance
Lightning Source LLC
LaVergne TN
LVHW072049060326
832903LV00053B/309